REFLECTIONS

COMPACT EDITION

INSPIRING AUSTRALIAN IMAGES BY KEN DUNCAN

In the middle of difficulty lies opportunity.

ALBERT EINSTEIN

REFLECTIONS

COMPACT EDITION

INSPIRING AUSTRALIAN IMAGES BY KEN DUNCAN

PANOGRAPHS®
PUBLISHING PTY LTD

THIS BOOK IS DEDICATED TO THE LORD GOD ALMIGHTY.
FOR WITHOUT HIS MAJESTIC CREATION, WE WOULD HAVE NOTHING TO REFLECT UPON.

INTRODUCTION

AT TIMES our lives become so very busy that we forget to pause and enjoy the beauty surrounding us. We allow the vortex of activity to consume us to the point where we no longer see things clearly. Our vision begins to blur. Soon there is nothing left in the whirl of our busyness but the hustle and bustle of our everyday lives. We find ourselves being driven by circumstances rather than taking time to consider our choices – and their likely consequences. At this point we need to realise, as Mahatma Gandhi once said, that there is much more to life than merely increasing its speed. It is so important we take time out to reflect on our lives and to look beyond ourselves. We need time to dream – time to recharge our batteries. Time to really live.

As a landscape photographer it is my constant privilege to travel through much that is beautiful in God's creation. In this I am very fortunate. My job is my passion – and what an office! Panoramic photography forces me to slow down and to look closely at the natural world. If I move too fast, I easily miss the message of a particular place. But if I pause long enough to properly experience a landscape, I begin to enter into a far bigger reality – a reality much more awesome than anything I dreamed possible.

Albert Einstein once said, "We should take care not to make the intellect our God – it has of course powerful muscles, but no personality." Instead our intellect and our experience of this world should be like a window into all that lies beyond. There is far more to our lives than the sum of our earthly existence. There is a Creator with a master plan and with infinite creative potential. Our being here on planet earth is not just an accident. The evidence is all around us. As one of my favourite Bible verses puts it: "For since the creation of the world God's invisible qualities – his eternal power and divine nature – have been clearly seen, being understood from what has been made, so that people are without excuse."

Australia is my home – a little piece of paradise on our awesome planet earth. Hopefully some of the images God has granted me, along with the accompanying collection of quotations, may help you reflect on the bigger picture God has for you. As a nation we may have our troubles, but it's never too late for change. Where there's life there's always hope. In fact, I believe there has never been a more important time for humanity to stop and reflect a while – for each of us to reassess our direction and purpose. As Gandhi said: "You must be the change you wish to see in the world." For it only takes a little light to dispel the darkness.

May God's love and light shine brightly upon you.

KEN DUNCAN, A FELLOW TRAVELLER.

Stumbling blocks are stepping stones to victory.

KEN DUNCAN

Remember that great love and great achievements involve great risk.

ANON

Life is what happens while we're busy making other plans.

JOHN LENNON

The journey gives meaning to the destination.

KEN DUNCAN

Now faith is being sure of what we hope for and certain of what we do not see.

HEBREWS 11:1

But those who hope in the LORD will renew their strength.

They will soar on wings like eagles; they will run and not grow weary, they will walk and not be faint.

ISAIAH 40:31

Never get so busy making a living that you forget to make a life.

ANON

Life can be tough, but we can be tougher.

KEN DUNCAN

I will refresh the weary and satisfy the faint.

JEREMIAH 31:25

Where there is love there is life.

MAHATMA GANDHI

Life is an adventure, not a worry.

KEN DUNCAN

Love comforts like sunshine after rain.

WILLIAM SHAKESPEARE

Hear my cry, O God; listen to my prayer.

From the ends of the earth I call to you,

I call as my heart grows faint; lead me to the rock that is higher than I.

For You have been my refuge, a strong tower against the foe.

I long to dwell in your tent forever and take refuge in the shelter of your wings.

PSALM 61:1-4

Faith is daring to go further than the eye can see.

ANON

This above all; to thine own self be true.

WILLIAM SHAKESPEARE

There are always flowers for those who want to see them.

HENRI MATISSE

How could drops of water know themselves to be a river?

Yet the river flows on.

ANTOINE DE SAINT-EXUPÉRY

Blessed is the man who perseveres under trial,

because when he has stood the test,

he will receive the crown of life that God has promised to those who love him.

JAMES 1:12

Silence is sometimes the best answer.

ANON

Life is about what we give, not about what we get.

KEN DUNCAN

For since the creation of the world God's invisible qualities—

his eternal power and divine nature—

have been clearly seen, being understood from what has been made,

so that men are without excuse.

ROMANS 1:20

There are only two ways to live your life.

One is as though nothing is a miracle.

The other is as though everything is a miracle.

ALBERT EINSTEIN

Many waters cannot quench love; rivers cannot wash it away.

SONG OF SONGS 8:7

What God has intended for you goes far beyond anything you can imagine.

OPRAH WINFREY

Those who bring sunshine to the lives of others cannot keep it from themselves.

JAMES MATTHEW BARRIE

Until you spread your wings, you'll have no idea how far you can fly.

ANON

A misty morning does not always signify a cloudy day.

ANON

This is courage in a man: to bear unflinchingly what heaven sends.

EURIPIDES

Choice, not chance, determines destiny.

ANON

If we don't change, we don't grow. If we don't grow, we aren't really living.

GAIL SHEEHY

The secret of success is constancy of purpose.

BENJAMIN DISRAELI

Love is a canvas furnished by Nature and embroidered by imagination.

VOLTAIRE

Be still, and know that I am God.

PSALM 46:10

There is more to life than increasing its speed.

MAHATMA GANDHI

There are no passengers on spaceship earth. We are all crew.

MARSHALL M^cLUHAN

If you're going through hell, keep going.

WINSTON CHURCHILL

As the purse is emptied, the heart is filled.

VICTOR HUGO

Human subtlety will never devise an invention more beautiful,
more simple or more direct than does Nature,
because in her inventions, nothing is lacking and nothing is superfluous.

LEONARDO DA VINCI

People only see what they are prepared to see.

RALPH WALDO EMERSON

He who endures, conquers.

PERSIUS

Some people cause happiness wherever they go; others whenever they go.

OSCAR WILDE

Peace I leave with you; my peace I give you.

I do not give to you as the world gives.

Do not let your hearts be troubled and do not be afraid.

JOHN 14:27

Great works are performed not by strength but by perseverance.

SAMUEL JOHNSON

Interestingly, according to modern astronomers, space is finite.

This is a very comforting thought – particularly for people who cannot remember where they left things.

WOODY ALLEN

Our greatest glory is not in never falling, but in rising every time we fall.

CONFUCIUS

Darkness cannot drive out darkness; only light can do that.

Hate cannot drive out hate; only love can do that.

MARTIN LUTHER KING, JR.

Possessions are like grains of sand; we can fill our pockets with them or share them to create a beautiful beach.

ANON

While we have life we have hope.

ANON

Trees are the earth's endless effort to speak to the listening heaven.

RABINDRANATH TAGORE

To stop giving is to stop living.

ANON

A generous soul is the home of paradise.

ANON

Not all who wander are lost.

J.R.R. TOLKIEN

Dreams are true while they last, and do we not live in dreams?

ALFRED TENNYSON

No pessimist ever discovered the secret of the stars,
or sailed to an uncharted land, or opened a new doorway for the human spirit.

HELEN KELLER

Do you not know? Have you not heard?

The LORD is the everlasting God, the Creator of the ends of the earth.

He will not grow tired or weary, and his understanding no-one can fathom.

He gives strength to the weary and increases the power of the weak.

ISAIAH 40:28-29

Anything will grow if it is appreciated.

ANON

Following the light of the sun, we left the Old World.

CHRISTOPHER COLUMBUS

As water will wear away rock, generous words will wear away the hardest heart.

ANON

Only the soul that loves is happy.

JOHANN WOLFGANG VON GOETHE

Our strength is in our roots.

KEN DUNCAN

The road to success is always under construction.

ARNOLD PALMER

The most beautiful thing we can experience is the mysterious.

ALBERT EINSTEIN

Look at everything as though you were seeing it for the first time or the last time.
Then your time on earth will be filled with glory.

BETTY SMITH

With a guiding light, all obstacles can be overcome.

ANON

May the God of hope fill you with all joy and peace as you trust in him,
so that you may overflow with hope by the power of the Holy Spirit.

ROMANS 15:13

All of our dreams can come true, if we have the courage to pursue them.

WALT DISNEY

What lies behind us and what lies before us are tiny matters compared to what lies within us.

RALPH WALDO EMERSON

He has the deed half done who has made a beginning.

HORACE

The best and most beautiful things in the world cannot be seen or even touched — they must be felt with the heart.

HELEN KELLER

Kind words can be short and easy to speak, but their echoes are truly endless.

MOTHER TERESA

Courage is its own reward.

PLAUTUS

Give thanks to the God of heaven. His love endures for ever.

PSALM 136:26

As long as you're going to think anyway, think big.

DONALD TRUMP

Deeds, not stones, are the true monuments of the great.

JOHN L. MOTLEY

Seize the day, put no trust in tomorrow.

HORACE

The man who has no imagination has no wings.

MUHAMMAD ALI

The path of the righteous is like the first gleam of dawn, shining ever brighter till the full light of day.

PROVERBS 4:18

No bird soars too high if he soars with his own wings.

WILLIAM BLAKE

We do not inherit this land from our ancestors; we borrow it from our children.

HAIDA INDIAN SAYING

The LORD said, "This far you may come and no farther; here is where your proud waves halt."

JOB 38:11

Time you enjoy wasting, was not wasted.

JOHN LENNON

REFLECTIONS COMPACT EDITION   First published 2007 by Panographs® Publishing Pty Ltd   ABN 21 050 235 606   PO Box 3015, Wamberal, NSW, 2260, Australia   Telephone +61 2 4367 6777   Email: panos@kenduncan.com   ©2007, Panographs® Publishing Pty Ltd   This publication is copyright. Other than for the purposes of and subject to the conditions prescribed under the Copyright Act 1968 (Commonwealth of Australia), no part of it in any form or by any means(electronic, mechanical, microcopying, photocopying, recording or otherwise) may be reproduced, stored in a retrieval system or transmitted without prior written permission of Panographs ®Publishing Pty Ltd.   Panographs® is a registered trademark of the Ken Duncan Group Pty Limited.   Photography by Ken Duncan   Text by Ken Duncan   ©2007 Divine Guidance P/L   Designed by Good Catch Design   Reprographics by CFL Print Studio   Printed and bound in China   The National Library of Australia Cataloguing-in-Publication entry: Duncan, Ken.   Reflections: inspiring Australian images.   Compact ed.   Includes index.   ISBN 9780977573042 (hbk.).   I. Photography, Panoramic - Australia. I. Title.   778.360994

To view the range of Ken Duncan's panoramic Limited Edition Prints visit the Ken Duncan Gallery online: **www.kenduncan.com**

INDEX TO IMAGES

I lift up my eyes to the hills — where does my help come from?

My help comes from the LORD, the Maker of heaven and earth.

PSALM 121:1-2